LEVEL
3

Skyscrapers

Libby Romero

NATIONAL
GEOGRAPHIC

Washington, D.C.

For Richard —L.R.

Published by National Geographic Partners, LLC, Washington, D.C. 20036. All rights reserved. Reproduction in whole or in part without written permission of the publisher is prohibited.

Library of Congress Cataloging-in-Publication Data

Names: Romero, Libby, author.
Title: National Geographic readers. Skyscrapers / Libby Romero.
Other titles: Skyscrapers
Description: Washington, DC : National Geographic Children's Books, 2017. |
  Series: National Geographic readers. Level 3
Identifiers: LCCN 2016038840 (print) | LCCN 2016038942 (ebook) | ISBN 9781426326813 (paperback) | ISBN 9781426326820 (hardcover) | ISBN 9781426326837 (e-book)
Subjects: LCSH: Skyscrapers—Juvenile literature. | BISAC: JUVENILE NONFICTION / Readers / Beginner.
Classification: LCC NA6230 .R56 2017 (print) | LCC NA6230 (ebook) | DDC 720/.483—dc23

LC record available at lccn.loc.gov/2016038840

The author and publisher gratefully acknowledge the expert content review of this book by Dr. Antony Wood, RIBA Ph.D., executive director, Council on Tall Buildings and Urban Habitat; and Marshall Gerometta, skyscraper database editor, Council on Tall Buildings and Urban Habitat; and the literacy review of this book by Mariam Jean Dreher, professor of reading education, University of Maryland, College Park.

Author's Note: Skyscrapers are a marvel of modern design. But they didn't appear out of the blue. Many other "firsts" made it possible for skyscrapers to exist. For example, the Flaxmill Maltings (1797) in Shrewsbury, England, was the first iron-framed building in the world. The Haughwout Building (1857) in New York City was the first commercial building with a safe passenger elevator. And the Cooper Union Foundation Building (1859) was one of the first buildings in New York to be supported by rolled wrought-iron beams. These buildings may not be skyscrapers, but they played a big part in history. They are the foundation upon which modern skyscrapers were built. On the cover, One World Trade Center towers over other buildings in New York City. Pictured on the title page in dense fog are the Shanghai World Financial Center, Jinmao Tower, and the Shanghai Tower in Pudong, Shanghai, China. The Table of Contents features the city central business district of Sydney, Australia.

National Geographic supports K–12 educators with ELA Common Core Resources.
Visit natgeoed.org/commoncore for more information.

Printed in the United States of America
16/WOR/1

Table of Contents

A History of Height

Throughout time, people have been fascinated with tall buildings. Ancient Egyptians built pyramids for their pharaohs. Later on, people built tall towers and giant cathedrals out of mortar and stone.

The largest pyramid in Giza, Egypt, was 481 feet tall when it was built.

Ulm Minster (530 feet) in Ulm, Germany, is the tallest church in the world.

But in the 1880s, two new ideas changed everything: One was using an iron-and-steel skeleton to support a building. The other was the invention of a safe passenger elevator. Now buildings could be bigger, taller, and stronger. The skyscraper was born.

Building Words

SKELETON: The supporting frame of something, like a building

SKYSCRAPER: A very tall building

Empire State Building (1,250 feet) in New York City

Famous Skyscrapers

THE CHICAGO BUILDING OF | THE HOME INSURANCE CO.
OF NEW YORK

People first used the word "skyscraper" to describe a building in 1885. That's what they called the Home Insurance Building in Chicago, Illinois, U.S.A. It was 10 stories (138 feet) tall and had an iron-and-steel skeleton. Since then, people's ideas about skyscrapers have changed.

Many skyscrapers are still built out of steel. But whether or not a building is called a skyscraper depends on how it compares to other buildings in the area. If a building stands out above other buildings, even if it is quite short, people could consider it to be a skyscraper.

Building Word

STORY: A floor of a skyscraper

The World's Smallest "Skyscraper"?

In 1919, a man named J. D. McMahon showed people plans for a high-rise building in Wichita Falls, Texas, U.S.A. He collected lots of money. But he didn't tell people that the plans showed the building measured in inches instead of feet. By the time people found out, it was too late. Their "skyscraper" was just four stories tall!

Newby-McMahon Building

Over time, there have been many famous skyscrapers. Some are famous because of their height. In 2017, the world's tallest skyscraper is the Burj Khalifa (berj kuh-LEE-fah) in Dubai, United Arab Emirates. It is 2,717 feet tall and has 163 floors!

Burj Khalifa

Other skyscrapers are famous because of their design. The Shanghai World Financial Center (1,614 feet) in China has a four-sided hole cut out of its top. Some people think the building looks like a giant bottle opener. And the Burj Al Arab (1,053 feet) in Dubai is shaped like a giant boat sail.

Burj Al Arab

Shanghai World Financial Center

Some skyscrapers are famous because they create a skyline that makes the city easy to recognize. Hong Kong is a great example. There are more skyscrapers here than anywhere else in the world. Other cities with famous skylines include New York City; Shanghai, China; Dubai, U.A.E.; and Sydney, Australia.

Building Word

SKYLINE: The outline of objects, such as buildings, against the background of the sky

Hong Kong skyline

Alain Robert is known as "the French Spiderman." He's climbed more than 100 skyscrapers—most using just his bare hands and chalk to keep his hands from slipping.

weird but true!

Why Build Skyscrapers?

When you see a giant skyscraper, one question you may ask is, "Why would people build something that tall?" The answer most likely has to do with money, space, and technology. That's why people first started building skyscrapers.

This drawing shows what Lower Manhattan looked like before skyscrapers and the fire of 1835.

New York's Great Fire of 1835 lasted for two days. Most of the destroyed buildings were businesses.

In the early 1800s, New York City became the finance center of the United States. But in 1835, a giant fire destroyed nearly 700 buildings in a section of the city called Manhattan. Everything had to be rebuilt.

Building Words

TECHNOLOGY: The use of scientific tools and methods for a practical reason

FINANCE: The business of managing money for a person, company, or government

But land was expensive. And more and more people kept moving to the city. There wasn't much space on the ground. So, they started to build upward.

The First Safe Passenger Elevator

People started using powered elevators in the 1830s. But these elevators weren't safe. If the cable broke, the elevator would fall to the ground. In 1853, Elisha Graves Otis invented a rope-break safety device. In 1857, the five-story E. V. Haughwout Building (79 feet) in New York became the first building to use Otis's passenger safety elevator. Thirteen years later, New York's seven-story Equitable Life Building (142 feet) became the first office building to have an elevator like this.

Elisha Graves Otis explains his elevator safety device.

Q Why did the new elevator refuse to go above the third floor?

A It was afraid of heights.

As they rebuilt, the people of New York were limited by technology. Bricks and mortar couldn't support the height and weight of very tall buildings. And who wanted to climb that many stairs, anyway? For these reasons, the tallest new building in New York in the 1850s was just five stories high.

By 1864, much of New York's financial district had been rebuilt.

While all this was going on in New York, the city of Chicago, Illinois, was also growing quickly. From 1830 to 1870, it grew from 50 people to nearly 300,000! Many people came for jobs. Because of Chicago's location in the middle of the United States, the city was a railroad center for the country. Much trade and business passed through the city.

But in 1871, fire tore through Chicago. More than 18,000 buildings were burned.

The Great Chicago Fire burned large parts of the city.

Making Steel

In 1856, English inventor Henry Bessemer discovered a new way to make steel. Before this, it was a slow, costly process. Bessemer invented a machine that made steel quickly. It could make big sheets of steel. And it was inexpensive.

By this time, both safe elevators and building materials made of iron and steel were available. Chicago was ready to build the world's first skyscraper!

Getting Off the Ground

Building a skyscraper takes more than steel, iron, and elevators. People also need a plan. Buildings must be built in a way that protects against gravity. Gravity can pull tall buildings to the ground.

Building Word

GRAVITY: The force that pulls objects toward the center of a planet or other body

The Woolworth Building (792 feet) in New York City is bigger on bottom than on top.

Ancient Egyptians built pyramids that had large bottoms and small tops. The bottom, or base, of a pyramid supports its weight. This helps pyramids fight against gravity. But these pyramids are in the middle of a desert. There's a lot of space there. In a city, there's less space and land is expensive. While this idea worked, it limited how tall new buildings could be built in a city.

The Giza Pyramids are more than 4,500 years old.

Workers have lunch on a steel beam during the construction of the RCA Building (850 feet) in New York City in 1932.

People needed a way to build a tall building with a smaller base. Steel made this possible. But steel beams were large and expensive. They had to be shipped in and stored. And people needed heavy-duty equipment to move them.

Because of this, some people made buildings out of concrete.

Many walls and floors are made of concrete. Concrete is solid and fireproof. It also blocks noise.

Concrete is a mixture of cement, sand, broken rocks, and water. It is cheaper than steel and it can be made on-site. Concrete gets very hard when it dries, so it can support a lot of weight. But concrete cracks if it's put under too much pressure. People needed a better idea. So they started to reinforce, or strengthen, concrete with steel bars.

Building With Reinforced Concrete

The 16-story Ingalls Building (180 feet) in Cincinnati, Ohio, U.S.A., was the world's first reinforced concrete skyscraper. It took builders two years to get permission to build this building. People didn't trust the concrete. They thought the building would collapse. But the reinforced concrete made the building strong. The Ingalls Building, completed in 1903, is still standing today!

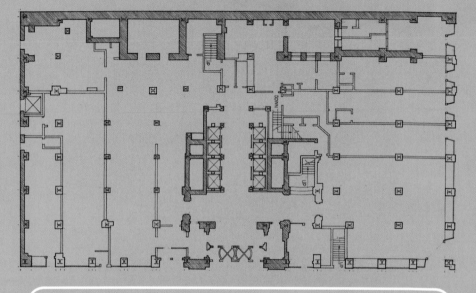

This illustration shows a floor plan of the Chicago Stock Exchange (187 feet), completed in 1894. Like other skyscrapers built before reinforced concrete was available, the rooms were very small.

New technologies didn't just help people build taller buildings. They also helped people solve problems inside. If a building's frame is made out of steel or reinforced concrete, its inner walls and floors help support it. This means the building's outer walls don't have to be as thick. And that leaves more space inside the building for bigger rooms.

Getting away from thick, solid, outer walls also solved the problem of light. Many older buildings were very dark. But now there could be more windows. Builders could even make the curtain wall, or outer covering of a skyscraper, out of glass.

Building Word

CURTAIN WALL: The outer covering of a skyscraper

modern office buildings in Brussels, Belgium

7 COOL FACTS
About Skyscrapers

1

The Empire State Building (1,250 feet) in New York City was the world's tallest skyscraper for 41 years. No other building has held that title longer.

2

People used to use the word "skyscraper" to describe anything tall that stuck up into the air. That included horses, people, and even hats!

3

In 2012, builders constructed the 30-story T30 skyscraper (328 feet) in Changsha, China, in just 15 days. They made all of the parts in advance. All they had to do was put them together.

In 2005, the helipad of the Burj Al Arab skyscraper (692 feet) in Dubai was temporarily changed into a tennis court. Andre Agassi and Roger Federer played an exhibition match there.

4

5

The elevators in the Shanghai Tower (2,073 feet) in Shanghai, China, can travel up to 46 miles an hour. They take people from the second-level basement to the 119th floor in less than a minute.

Before safe elevators were invented, people wanted to rent space on the lower floors of tall buildings. After elevators, people paid more for the top floors, which had better views.

6

7

On August 7, 1974, Frenchman Philippe Petit put a steel cable between the two towers of the World Trade Center in New York City. For 45 minutes, he walked across the cable that was 1,300 feet off the ground.

Working With Nature

ground level

steel column

concrete cap

concrete support

solid ground

STEP 1: A strong base is needed when building a skyscraper.

When building a skyscraper, people must think about nature. The first thing to consider is the ground below. You need a strong, stable base. So when people build a skyscraper today, they dig until they hit hard, solid ground. They fill the holes with concrete to build supports. They put concrete caps on the supports.

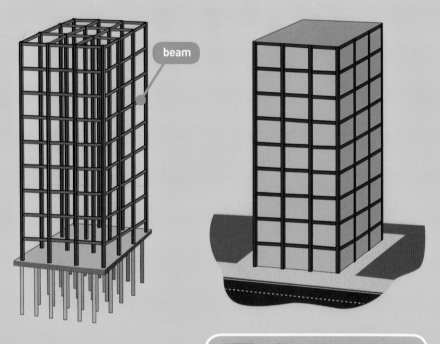

beam

STEP 2: Columns and beams make the building's skeleton.

STEP 3: Glass, stone, concrete, and other materials cover the outside of the building.

Once the base is sturdy, they start to build up. They make a skeleton out of concrete, steel, or a combination of these materials. Columns go up. Beams go across on each floor. The strong base and strong skeleton work together to help the skyscraper resist the natural force of gravity.

Builders must also consider the weather. Changes in temperature, for example, can affect metals. Metals expand when temperatures are hot and contract when they are cold. Over time, this can cause metals to crack or change shape.

Wind can cause problems, too. Wind moves skyscrapers back and forth. Skyscrapers must be strong. But they must also be flexible. If the tall buildings don't move when the wind blows, pressure from the wind will damage them. To keep this from happening, builders sometimes cross steel beams between columns like an X. The X's brace the building against the wind.

Building Words

EXPAND: To pull apart and get bigger

CONTRACT: To push together and get smaller

New York's Empire State Building (1,250 feet) was completed in 1931. It was designed to be a giant lightning rod for the surrounding area. It gets struck by lightning about 23 times every year!

Skyscraper Design

In the 1960s, engineer Fazlur R. Khan thought of a new way to build skyscrapers. He connected giant tubes, or columns, of steel to make one big building with several giant sections. The Willis Tower (1,451 feet, and formerly the Sears Tower) in Chicago, Illinois, was built in 1974. It is made of nine tubes. The tubes support one another and work together to make the building strong. The tubes are different heights. This breaks up the force of the wind as it blows on the building.

Earthquakes are another big problem for buildings. Earthquakes make the ground move. This can cause buildings to get badly damaged. Builders add parts to skyscrapers to try to keep this from happening.

Minimizing Movement

Taipei 101 is a 1,667-foot-tall skyscraper in Taipei, Taiwan. This photo shows the skyscraper's giant steel damper between the 92nd and 87th floors. A damper is a part that helps the skyscraper sway less during an earthquake or strong winds. This damper is 18 feet across and weighs 728 tons.

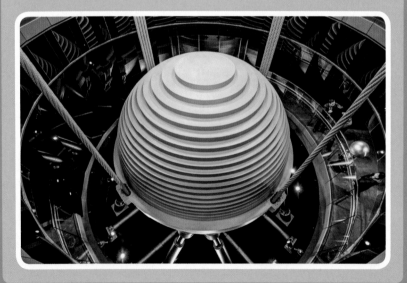

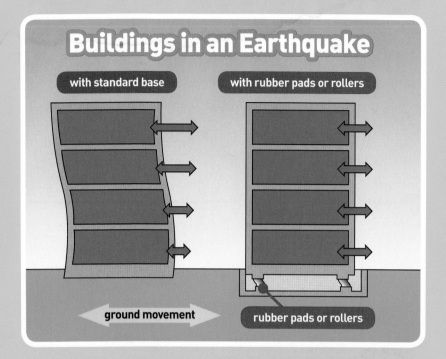

Buildings in an Earthquake

with standard base

with rubber pads or rollers

ground movement

rubber pads or rollers

Sometimes builders use dampers or other parts called shock absorbers. These parts keep the skyscraper steady and limit movement in an earthquake. Builders can also put rubber pads and rollers between a skyscraper and its base. These parts move sideways during an earthquake. They carry the weight of the building with them. So the building moves, but it doesn't fall over.

Going Green

Grattacielo Intesa Sanpaolo (545 feet) in Turin, Italy, is an energy-saving green building.

Big buildings use lots of energy. Since the year 2000, people have designed skyscrapers that use less energy. They have also found ways to save energy in skyscrapers that were already built. One simple idea is to change the lightbulbs. New types of lightbulbs use less energy than old ones.

New energy-saving lightbulbs can use 70–90 percent less energy than other lightbulbs.

Another way to save energy is to replace the windows. At one time, all skyscrapers had windows that didn't open. Now many do open. This means natural air can help cool the buildings instead of only using air conditioning. The windows are also tinted like sunglasses. They reflect light and heat. So people use much less electricity to control the temperature inside.

Windows open to cool the air in Manitoba Hydro Place (377 feet) in Winnipeg, Manitoba, Canada.

Big buildings also use a lot of water. An easy way to save water is to update the faucets and fixtures people use to get water. Newer fixtures use less water. So the owners replaced the fixtures at Taipei 101 (1,667 feet). Now people in the building save 7.4 million gallons of drinkable water each year.

Taipei 101

Some buildings don't just save water. They save energy by using water in different ways. There's a three-story waterfall in the Hearst Tower (597 feet) in New York City. The water comes from rain outside. The waterfall cools the area inside.

The waterfall in the Hearst Tower flows around escalators.

Hearst Tower

Some skyscrapers make their own energy. The Pearl River Tower (1,015 feet) in Guangzhou Province, China, does this with wind. The building has four giant openings. As wind moves through the openings, giant turbines inside the building turn to make energy.

Giant openings let air flow through the Pearl River Tower.

Building Word

TURBINE: An engine with a part that has blades. The blades spin when water, air, or steam moves past them.

Some skyscrapers use nature in different ways. Bosco Verticale, or "vertical forest" in Italian, is the name of two skyscrapers (380 feet and 279 feet) in Milan, Italy. These skyscrapers are covered with plants and trees. The plants make oxygen and reduce smog. They also block outside noise and help keep the buildings cool.

The balconies of Bosco Verticale hold hundreds of trees and plants.

37

What's Up With Skyscrapers Now?

Many things have changed since the world's first skyscraper was built. One thing is location. For many years, most of the tallest buildings were in North America. Not anymore.

Today, the world's tallest buildings are rising in Asia and the Middle East. That's because these places have lots of people and open land. They also have the money to build tall skyscrapers.

Shanghai, China, skyline in 2015

Petronas Twin Towers
(1,483 feet) in
Kuala Lumpur, Malaysia

Chrysler Building
(1,046 feet) in New York City

One World Trade Center
(1,776 feet) in New York City

Another thing that has changed since the first skyscrapers were built is height. Today, skyscrapers are much taller than they used to be.

The first building to change people's ideas about height was the Chrysler Building in New York. Completed in 1930, it won the title of "World's Tallest Building." It was the first "supertall" skyscraper ever built. Today, any building taller than 984 feet (the height of the Eiffel Tower in Paris, France) is called a supertall. There are now more than 100 supertalls.

weird but true!

In 2013, sunlight bounced off of the windows of a skyscraper in London, England. It was so hot that it melted parts of a car!

Walkie Talkie Building (525 feet) in London, England

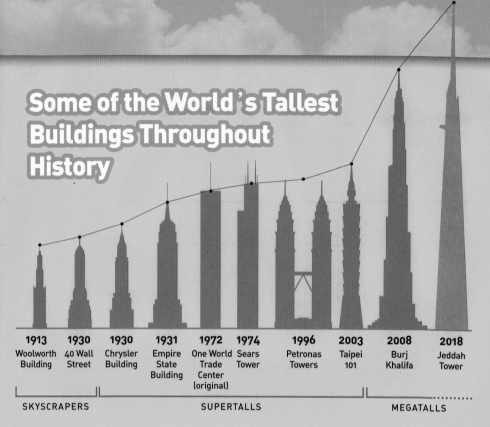

Some of the World's Tallest Buildings Throughout History

1913	1930	1930	1931	1972	1974	1996	2003	2008	2018
Woolworth Building	40 Wall Street	Chrysler Building	Empire State Building	One World Trade Center (original)	Sears Tower	Petronas Towers	Taipei 101	Burj Khalifa	Jeddah Tower

SKYSCRAPERS   SUPERTALLS   MEGATALLS

But supertall doesn't seem to be tall enough anymore. People have started to build "megatall" skyscrapers. These buildings, which are at least 1,968 feet tall, are more than twice as tall as the shortest supertall.

For now, just three megatalls rule the skies. But that will change. Builders hope to finish the Jeddah Tower in Jeddah, Saudi Arabia, in 2018. It will be at least 3,281 feet tall! The sky isn't the limit anymore.

This illustration shows what the Jeddah Tower will look like when it's finished.

QUIZ WHIZ

How much do you know about skyscrapers? After reading this book, probably a lot! Take this quiz and find out.
Answers are at the bottom of page 45.

When was the word "skyscraper" first used to describe a building?

A. 1607
B. 1885
C. 1903
D. 1972

1

2

What two inventions made it possible to build skyscrapers?

A. steel and glass
B. iron and steel
C. steel and elevators
D. concrete and glass

The _____ is the supporting frame of a skyscraper.

A. curtain wall
B. story
C. skyline
D. skeleton

3

4

As of 2017, _____ is the tallest skyscraper.

A. the Empire State Building
B. the Home Insurance Building
C. Burj Khalifa
D. Taipei 101

In which city was the first skyscraper built?

5

A. Chicago, Illinois, U.S.A.
B. New York City, U.S.A.
C. Shanghai, China
D. Dubai, United Arab Emirates

6

What is a skyscraper called that is taller than 984 feet?

A. megatall
B. supertall
C. mightytall
D. verytall

7

Where are most of the skyscrapers being built today?

A. North America and South America
B. Europe and Asia
C. Australia and Africa
D. Asia and the Middle East

Answers: 1) B, 2) C, 3) D, 4) C, 5) A, 6) B, 7) D

Glossary

CONTRACT: To push together and get smaller

FINANCE: The business of managing money for a person, company, or government

GRAVITY: The force that pulls objects toward the center of a planet or other body

SKYSCRAPER: A very tall building

STORY: A floor of a skyscraper

CURTAIN WALL: The outer covering of a skyscraper

EXPAND: To pull apart and get bigger

SKELETON: The supporting frame of something, like a building

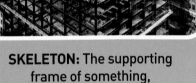

SKYLINE: The outline of objects, such as buildings, against the background of the sky

TECHNOLOGY: The use of scientific tools and methods for a practical reason

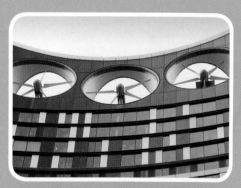

TURBINE: An engine with a part that has blades. The blades spin when water, air, or steam moves past them.